Guided Reading Notes

Light Blue Band
Oxford Level 4

Bugs

Contents

Introduction	2
The Race (Fiction)	6
Ant's Bug Adventure (Fiction)	13
Zak and Zee (Fiction)	20
Bug Hunt (Non-fiction)	27
What Do Bugs Eat? (Non-fiction)	34

Introduction

Why is guided reading important?

Guided reading plays an important role in your whole-school provision for reading, providing opportunities for children to progress and develop the key competencies they need to become confident and skilled independent readers. Working with small groups of children, with texts closely matched to the readers' needs, guided reading is the perfect vehicle for delivering focused teaching from Reception/Pl right through to Year 6/P7. The teacher-pupil interaction also provides a valuable assessment opportunity, helping you identify exactly what each child can and can't do. Through guided reading children also encounter a world of exciting, whole books – building a community of readers who read for pleasure.

About *Project X Origins*

Project X Origins is a comprehensive, whole-school guided reading programme designed to help you teach the wide range of skills essential to ensure children progress as readers and to help nurture a love of reading.

Ensuring the key skills are covered

Project X Origins incorporates all of the key skills children need to develop to become successful and enthusiastic readers:

> **Word reading:** phonically regular and common exception words are introduced systematically in the early levels with phonic opportunities provided throughout the notes. As children progress, they are encouraged to use their decoding skills whenever they encounter new or unfamiliar words, and also to recognize how this impacts on different spelling rules.

> **Comprehension:** understanding what has been read is central to being an effective and engaged reader but comprehension is not something that comes automatically so specific strategies have been built into the notes to ensure children develop comprehension skills they can use over a range of texts:

- Previewing
- Predicting
- Activating and building prior knowledge
- Questioning
- Recalling
- Visualizing and other sensory responses
- Deducting, inferring and drawing conclusions
- Determining importance
- Synthesizing
- Empathizing
- Summarizing
- Personal response, including adopting a critical response

> **Reading fluency:** fluency occurs as children develop automatic word recognition, reading with pace and expression. Strategies to help achieve this, including meaningful opportunities for oral reading, re-reading and re-listening are provided throughout.

> **Vocabulary:** introducing new vocabulary within a meaningful context is an important element in extending children's vocabulary range, developing their reading fluency and comprehension. Each thematic cluster provides opportunities for revisiting and reinforcing vocabulary over a range of books and contexts.

> **Grammar, punctuation and spelling:** learning about language in the context of a text, rather than through a series of discrete exercises, can help make grammar, punctuation and spelling relevant and helps children make the link between grammar, punctuation and clarity of meaning, thus supporting their development as writers. Opportunities to support an in-depth look at language are provided for every book from Year 1/P2 to Year 6/P7.

> **Spoken language:** talk is crucial to learning and developing their comprehension so children are given plenty of opportunities to: discuss and debate their ideas with others; justify their opinions; ask and answer questions; explore and hypothesise; summarise, describe and explain; and listen and respond to the ideas of others.

Assessment and progression in reading

Project X Origins includes a rigorous assessment spine drawn from the *Oxford Ros Wilson Reading Criterion Scale* to ensure that you know exactly what each child can do and what they need to focus on next in order to make progress. This assessment framework, combined with the careful levelling of the Oxford Levels, will help you select the right book with the right level of challenge for each of your guided reading groups and to assess, track and monitor each child's progress.

Step 1

On a termly basis, use the *Reading Criterion Scale* (which can be found in the relevant *Project X Origins Teaching Handbook*) to assess each child's reading. The scale will tell you the Oxford Level a child is comfortable reading at, and the areas a child needs to develop. You can also use this assessment to form your guided reading groups.

Step 2

Plan your guided reading sessions by selecting books at the appropriate Oxford Level that focus on the relevant learning needs of the group. You will find charts showing the learning objectives and assessment points for every *Project X Origins* book in the relevant *Project X Origins Teaching Handbook*. Depending on your assessment, you might choose a book at the level the children are comfortable at or one from the next level up, to offer some stretch.

Step 3

Use the assessment points within the Guided Reading Notes to support on-going assessment of children's reading progress. The Progress Tracking Charts in the relevant *Project X Origins Teaching Handbook* can be used to record this if you wish. Regularly re-assess each child's progress combining your on-going informal assessments and the termly assessment using the *Reading Criterion Scale*. Use this information to re-organize guided reading groups and teaching plans in response to children's varying degrees of progress.

Getting started: using the Guided Reading Notes

At a glance
Project X Origins Guided Reading Notes offer detailed guidance to help deliver effective and engaging guided reading sessions, and are designed to be used flexibly to ensure you get the most out of each book. For notes containing multiple sessions, you may choose to focus on each of these sessions or focus on one session and have the children read the rest of the book independently.

Curricula correlation and assessment
At the beginning of every set of notes there are correlation charts for all UK curricula, ensuring that across the clusters the main curricula objectives are covered. In addition, an overview of assessment points for each book is provided – these points are also signposted throughout the notes.

Key information
Before the first session, an overview of the book and the resources you will need (such as additional photocopy masters) is provided.

Teaching sequence
Each guided reading session follows the same teaching sequence:
- **Before reading**: children explore the context of each book to support their understanding and help them engage with the text. They are encouraged to discuss, recall, respond, predict and speculate about the book. Opportunities to focus on word reading and/or vocabulary are also introduced at this point.
- **During reading**: children are given a section of the book to read with specific questions in mind.
- **After reading**: children reflect on and discuss what they have read. They are encouraged to delve deeper, exploring their understanding of the text, developing their vocabulary, grammar, punctuation, spelling and fluency where appropriate.
- **Follow-up**: opportunities for children to extend their learning outside the session are provided, including writing and cross-curricular activities.

Throughout the sessions, the key strategies that children are developing are clearly identified.

The Race
BY TONY BRADMAN

Curricula correlation

English National Curriculum

Spoken language	Articulate and justify answers, arguments and opinions
Word reading	Read words containing taught GPCs and -ed endings
Comprehension	Predict what might happen on the basis of what has been read so far
	Make inferences on the basis of what is being said and done
	Explain clearly their understanding of what is read to them

Phonics and vocabulary

GPCs	/ai/ snail, fails, waiting /ng/ waiting, winning, going, playing
Decodable words (Phase 4)	going, buttons, rocket, ever, never, waiting, winning, snail, sure, fails, grin, with, trees
Common exception words	said, what, do, looked, like, there, so
Challenge and context words	race, happy, micro-buggy, idea, secret, dragonfly, day-dreamed, play, time

Developing grammar, punctuation and spelling

Grammar and Punctuation	How words can combine to make sentences	Cat and Tiger pushed the buttons.
Spelling	Words ending -y	micro-buggy, only, ready, steady, very, happy

Reading assessment points

Word reading	Can the children use phonic knowledge to attempt unknown words?
Comprehension	Are the children beginning to make predictions based on titles, text, blurb and/or pictures?
	Can the children, with support, find information to help answer simple, literal questions, in texts at an appropriate reading level?
	Can the children retell known stories, including significant events/main ideas in sequence?
	Can the children notice interesting words?

Scottish Curriculum for Excellence

Listening and talking	When I engage with others, I know when and how to listen, when to talk, how much to say, when to ask questions and how to respond with respect LIT 1-02a
Reading	I am learning to select and use strategies and resources, before I read and as I read, to help make the meaning of texts clear LIT 1-13a

Welsh National Literacy Framework

Oracy	Include some detail and some relevant vocabulary to extend their ideas or accounts (Speaking)
Reading	Apply the following reading strategies with increasing independence: phonic strategies to decode words, recognition of high-frequency words, context clues, e.g. prior knowledge, graphic and syntactic clues, and self-correction, including re-reading and reading ahead (Reading strategies)
	Retell events from a narrative in the right order (Comprehension)
	Explore language, information and events in texts (Response and analysis)

Northern Ireland Curriculum

Talking and Listening	Express themselves with increasing clarity and confidence, using a growing vocabulary and more complex sentence structure
Reading	Use extended vocabulary when discussing text, retelling stories or in their emergent writing
	Make and give reasons for predictions

The Race

About this book

Cat and Tiger have a race. Tiger has the micro-buggy but Cat only has a snail. Although Tiger is fast he day-dreams while Cat keeps going. She wins.

You will need

- *Sequencing The Race* Photocopy Master, *Teaching Handbook* for Year 1/P2

> Before reading

- Look closely at the picture on the cover. Ask the children what they can see. What are Cat and Tiger doing? **(activating prior knowledge)**
- Read the title. Discuss any ideas the children have about what might happen in the story. **(predicting)**

Assessment point

Are the children beginning to make predictions based on titles, text, blurb and/or pictures?

> Phonic opportunity

- Draw attention to words with the /ai/ phoneme: *snail, fails, waiting*. Ask the children to identify the GPC /ai/ in the words. Support children to say each phoneme and then blend the phonemes to read the word. Ask children to think of other words with the /ai/ sound. Now do the same for the /ng/ phoneme: *waiting, winning, going, playing*
- Alternatively, depending on the phonic work you have been undertaking, select one or two of the words from the book and remind the children how to say and blend phonemes.
- You may also wish to point out some of the common exception words, or practise decoding some of the challenge and context words in this book.

Assessment point

Can the children use phonic knowledge to attempt unknown words?

- Depending on your usual practice and the group you are working with, you may wish to:
  - Share the book with the children before they read it themselves. Read the first few pages together and ask the children to read the rest independently. In this case pause after page 5 and ask the children how Cat might be feeling when Tiger makes fun of her sledge. **(empathizing)** Then read pages 6 and 7 to support the children with the more challenging vocabulary: *smoke, ready* and *steady*. Briefly look at pages 12 and 14 to focus on *day-dreamed* and *secret*. Afterwards ask the children to read the book independently.
  - Invite the children to read the whole book independently.

During reading

- If you have not already done so, ask the children what to do if they encounter a difficult word, modelling with an example from the book if necessary. Remind the children of the more challenging vocabulary which you looked at before reading the book. Praise children who successfully decode unfamiliar words.
- As you listen to individual children read, you may wish to ask some of the following questions to check their understanding of the story:
  - What are Cat and Tiger doing? (pp.4–5)
  - Why does Tiger say "*You will only see my smoke*"? (pp.6–7)
  - What was Tiger day-dreaming about? (p.12)
- Ask the children to look out for words that end in *-y*.

Assessment point
Can the children, with support, find information to help answer simple, literal questions, in texts at an appropriate reading level?

After reading

Returning to the text

- Ask the children to take it in turns to tell the group what they thought of the story. Which part did they enjoy most? Why? Encourage the children to respond to each other's comments. **(personal response)**
- Ask the children to tell you briefly what happened in the story. **(recall, summarizing)**
- Ask the children to explain why Tiger thought he would win. **(deducing, inferring)**
- Why do the children think Cat won in the end? **(recall, deducing, inferring, drawing conclusions)**

> **Assessment point**
> Can the children retell known stories, including significant events/main ideas in sequence?

Developing comprehension

- Ask the children to imagine how Tiger felt when he lost the race. Have the children ever lost a race? How did they feel? **(empathizing)**
- Challenge children to order the pictures on the *Sequencing The Race* Photocopy Master and add sentences to them, either orally or in writing. **(summarizing)**

Developing vocabulary

- Look back at the text and read some of the pages again, e.g. pages 2–4, 5–6, and 12–13. What do the children notice about some of the words? (They rhyme, e.g. *do/too, joke/smoke, grin/win*.)

Assessment point
Can the children notice interesting words?

Developing grammar, punctuation and spelling

- Pick out a sentence and explore how the sentence has been created by combining words in an order that makes sense, e.g. subject, verb, object. Reorder the words to show how they would not make sense in a different order. Look further at how the sentences are in an order to build up understanding, rather than written in a random order. Make links to the children's own writing.
- Look at the words the children have found ending -*y*. Discuss how in some words the -*y* makes the /ee/ sound, e.g. *happy, very*, but in others it makes a different sound, e.g. /igh/ in *by*. Discuss how they are both spelt with -*y* but make different sounds.

"This micro-buggy is so fast. You will only see my smoke!"

"Race you to the tree!" said Tiger. "Ready, steady, here we go!"

Follow-up

Writing activities

- Encourage the children to imagine themselves in the role of Cat. What object and minibeast would the children use to make a 'racing buggy'? Why would they choose that object or minibeast? The children could draw a picture of it and label it. **(short writing task)**
- The children could use some of the pictures from the *Sequencing The Race* Photocopy Master to write part of the story. **(longer writing task)**

Other literacy activities

- Read the story of 'The Hare and the Tortoise' and discuss similarities with this story. **(spoken language)**

Cross-curricular activities

- Design/make a 'racing buggy'. **(Art and Design, DT)**
- Children could do some research about snails using simple information books or the Internet. They could then write/draw two facts about snails. **(Science)**
- Go on a snail hunt and investigate snail trails to find out more about snails and their habitat. **(Science)**
- Use thumb prints, potato prints or string to make pictures of snails. **(Art and Design)**
- Play snail hopscotch by drawing a huge snail shell with the squares of the hopscotch coiling into the middle and numbered one to twenty. Starting at the outside of the shell, throw a small pebble on to the first square, then hop in the square, pick up the pebble and hop out again. Continue this way, right through to the end square, just as if the children were playing an ordinary game of hopscotch. **(Maths, PE)**

Ant's Bug Adventure
BY JAN BURCHETT AND SARA VOGLER

Curricula correlation
English National Curriculum

Spoken language	Give well-structured descriptions and explanations
Word reading	Read common exception words
Comprehension	Link what they read or hear read to their own experiences
	Understand books by discussing the significance of events

Phonics and vocabulary

Adjacent consonants	fast, flash, stag, black, jump, help
Decodable words (Phase 4)	button, faster, pointed, landed, fast, flash, stag, black, jump, help, shook, again
Common exception words	said, were, out
Challenge and context words	beetle, scary, walk, talk, photo, watch, jaws, inside, suddenly

Developing grammar, punctuation and spelling

Grammar and Punctuation	Sequencing sentences to form short narratives	Throughout but good example on page 10
Spelling	Adding -ing, -ed, -er to verbs (where no change is needed to the root word)	bored, looked, pushed, yelled, jumped, landed, picked

Reading assessment points

Word reading	Can children use knowledge of letters, sounds and words to establish meaning when reading aloud?
Comprehension	Can children talk about likes/dislikes of stories and information texts?
	Can the children answer simple questions/find information in response to a direct, literal question?
	Can the children make plausible predictions about characters, using knowledge of the story, own experiences, etc?

Scottish Curriculum for Excellence

Listening and talking	I can select ideas and relevant information, organise these in a logical sequence and use words which will be interesting and/or useful for others LIT 1-06a
Reading	To show my understanding, I can respond to different kinds of questions and other close reading tasks and I am learning to create some questions of my own. ENG 1-17a
	I can share my thoughts about structure, characters and/or setting, recognise the writer's message and relate it to my own experiences, and comment on the effective choice of words and other features ENG 1-19a

Welsh National Literacy Framework

Oracy	Express an opinion on familiar subjects (Speaking)
Reading	Apply the following reading strategies with increasing independence: phonic strategies to decode words, recognition of high-frequency words, context clues, e.g. prior knowledge, graphic and syntactic clues, and self-correction, including re-reading and reading ahead (Reading strategies)
	Use personal experience to support understanding of texts (Comprehension)

Northern Ireland Curriculum

Talking and Listening	Express themselves with increasing clarity and confidence, using a growing vocabulary and more complex sentence structure
Reading	Make and give reasons for predictions

About this book
Ant makes himself small to look inside a log and sees a stag beetle.

You will need
- *Match the picture* Photocopy Master, *Teaching Handbook* for Year 1/P2
- *What does Ant think, feel, say?* Photocopy Master, *Teaching Handbook* for Year 1/P2
- Pictures of a stag beetle, millipede, ladybird and a snail

Ant's Bug Adventure

▷ Before reading

- Look closely at the picture on the cover of the book. Ask the children what they can see. What are Ant and his dad doing? **(previewing the text)**
- Read the title. Discuss any ideas of what might happen in this story. **(predicting)**
- If possible, look at some pictures of minibeasts, e.g. stag beetle, millipede, ladybird, snail. Alternatively, use the pictures from the *Match the picture* Photocopy Master. Do the children know the names of the minibeasts? Have the children seen any of these minibeasts before? **(activating prior knowledge)**

▷ *Phonic opportunity*

- Draw attention to words with adjacent consonants: *black, stag, fast, jump, help*. Read one of the words, sound it out and demonstrate how to blend the adjacent consonants. Ask the children to identify and blend the consonant sounds in the other words.
- Alternatively, depending on the phonic work you have been undertaking, select one or two of the words from the book and remind the children how to say and blend phonemes.
- You may also wish to point out some of the common exception words, or practise decoding some of the challenge and context words in this book.

15

- Depending on your usual practice and the group you are working with, you may wish to:
  - Share the book with the children before they read it themselves. Read the first few pages together and ask the children to read the rest independently. In this case, read pages 4 and 5 to the children using expression. Then ask the children to read the book independently.
  - Invite the children to read the whole book independently.

During reading

- If you have not already done so, ask the children what to do if they encounter a difficult word. Praise children who successfully decode unfamiliar words.
- As you listen to individual children read, you may wish to ask some of the following questions to check their understanding of the story:
  - What does Ant think? (p.4)
  - Why does he think this? (p.4)
  - What does Ant see in the log? (p.8)
  - Why does Ant point his watch at the stag beetle? (p.12)
  - What does Ant say to the stag beetle? (p.16)
- Ask the children to look for verbs (action words) ending -ed as they read.

Assessment point
- Can the children use knowledge of letters, sounds and words to establish meaning when reading aloud?

Assessment point
Can the children answer simple questions/find information in response to a direct, literal question?

After reading

Returning to the text

- Ask the children what they thought of the story. Which part did they enjoy most? Why? **(personal response)**
- Ask the children to tell you briefly what happened in the story. **(recall, summarizing)**
- Can the children explain why Ant was bored? **(deducing, inferring)**
- Encourage the children to discuss how Ant felt when he saw all the bugs. **(deducing, inferring, drawing conclusions, empathizing)**

> **Assessment point**
> Can the children talk about likes/dislikes of stories and information texts?

Developing comprehension

- Ask the children to imagine what Ant was thinking and feeling when he was chased by the stag beetle. Use the *What does Ant think, feel, say?* Photocopy Master. How would the children feel if they were chased by the stag beetle? What would they do? **(empathizing, visualizing)**

> **Assessment point**
> Can the children make plausible predictions about characters, using knowledge of the story, own experiences, etc?

Suddenly the log shook. Ant saw a big, dark shape. He was amazed. It was a stag beetle.

The beetle was black with big jaws.
"Yikes!" said Ant. "I will use my watch to take a photo."

Developing vocabulary

- Look at page 11 and read the description of the beetle: *The beetle was black with big jaws.* What do the children notice about some of the words? Rearrange the words, e.g. *big black beetle* and explain that this is an example of alliteration. Ask the children to talk with a partner to see if, together, they can make up a similar phrase for some other minibeasts (ladybird, ant, spider, snail, millipede).

Developing grammar, punctuation and spelling

- Ask children to reread pages 4–5 and identify how the sentences are sequenced to form short narratives. Make links to their own writing.
- Look at the words the children have found ending *-ed*. Discuss how the suffix *-ed* can be added to some verbs, without changing the root word, e.g. *push–pushed*. Discuss that the addition of *-ed* shows that something has happened in the past.

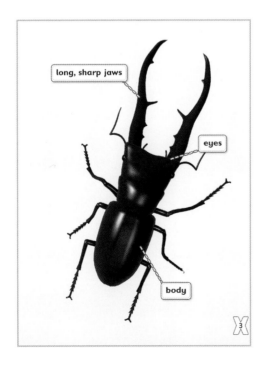

Developing fluency

- Ask one of the children to role play being Ant and invite the other children to ask 'him' questions based on the experiences shown in the book. **(questioning, empathizing)**

Follow-up

Writing activities

- Using the *Match the picture* Photocopy Master match the silhouette to the picture of the minibeast and write the name of the minibeast. **(short writing task)**
- Write the story on a computer using clip art and speech bubbles. **(longer writing task)**

Other literacy activities

- Watch the story on the Project X *Interactive Stories* software.

Cross-curricular activities

- Children could do some research about stag beetles using simple information books or the Internet. They could then write/draw two facts about stag beetles. **(Science)**
- Create an environment (log pile) to encourage stag beetles and other minibeasts. **(Science)**
- Make a minibeast collage using paper, scraps of material, etc. **(Art and Design)**
- Use clay/modelling materials to make a small sculpture of a minibeast. **(Art and Design)**

Zak and Zee
BY JEANNE WILLIS

Curricula correlation

English National Curriculum

Spoken language	Ask relevant questions to extend their understanding and build vocabulary and knowledge
Word reading	Apply phonic knowledge and skills as the route to decode words
Comprehension	Understand books by discussing the significance of the title and events
	Make inferences on the basis of what is being said and done
	Explain clearly their understanding of what is read to them

Phonics and vocabulary

GPCs	/er/ bigger, another, wonder /ear/ ear, hear
Decodable words (Phase 4)	bigger, green, just, hear, still, tail, small, another
Common exception words	one, were, out, said, do, like, come, some, have, so
Challenge and context words	eyes, very, dragonfly, face, flew, play

Developing grammar, punctuation and spelling

Grammar and Punctuation	Capital letters for names and the personal pronoun I	Zak Bug, Zee Bug, I, Zak, Zee
Spelling	The sound /ee/ spelt as ee, ea, and e	Zee, tree, see, tea, me

Reading assessment points

Word reading	Can the children use phonic knowledge to attempt unknown words?
	Can the children read aloud and begin to use expression to show awareness of punctuation?
Comprehension	Can the children make predictions based on the title, text, blurb and pictures?
	Can the children retell known stories, including significant events/main ideas in sequence?
	Can the children make plausible predictions about characters, using knowledge of the story, own experiences, etc.?

Scottish Curriculum for Excellence

Listening and talking	I am exploring how pace, gesture, expression, emphasis and choice of words are used to engage others, and I can use what I learn ENG I-03a
Reading	I am learning to select and use strategies and resources, before I read and as I read, to help make the meaning of texts clear LIT I-13a

Welsh National Literacy Framework

Oracy	Retell narratives or information that they have heard (Listening)
Reading	Apply the following reading strategies with increasing independence: phonic strategies to decode words, recognition of high-frequency words, context clues, e.g. prior knowledge, graphic and syntactic clues, and self-correction, including re-reading and reading ahead (Reading strategies)
	Read aloud with attention to full stops and question marks (Reading strategies)

Northern Ireland Curriculum

Talking and Listening	Retell stories, events or personal experiences in sequence with reasonable detail
	Begin to read with expression in response to print variations and punctuation
Reading	Use a range of reading cues with increasing independence and begin to self-correct

Zak and Zee

About this book

Zee Bug cannot see very well. He meets Zak Bug but doesn't realize he's talking to his back. In the end they both fly off together.

You will need

- *Match the rhyming words* Photocopy Master, *Teaching Handbook* for Year 1/P2
- *Zak and Zee* Photocopy Master, *Teaching Handbook* for Year 1/P2
- Pictures of bugs with eye markings, e.g. butterflies (peacock butterfly, owl butterfly), moths (eyed hawk-moth)

Before reading

- Look at the cover together, reading the title and the back cover blurb and looking closely at the pictures. What can the children see? What do the children think is going to happen in the story? **(activating prior knowledge, predicting)**

Assessment point

Can children make predictions based on the title, text, blurb and pictures?

Phonic opportunity

- Draw attention to words with the /er/ phoneme: *bigger, another, wonder*. Ask children to identify the GPC /er/ in the words. Support children to say each phoneme and then blend the phonemes to read the word. Ask children to think of other words with the /er/ sound. Now do the same for the /ear/ phoneme: *ear, hear*.
- Alternatively, depending on the phonic work you have been undertaking, select one or two of the words from the book and remind the children how to say and blend phonemes.
- You may also wish to point out some of the common exception words, or practise decoding some of the challenge and context words in this book.

Assessment point

Can the children use phonic knowledge to attempt unknown words?

- Look at pages 2 and 3. Ask the children to describe the two bugs. What is special about Zak Bug? Why does he have 'eye' markings on his back? If possible, show the children some pictures of other insects that have 'eye' markings, e.g. peacock butterfly, eyed hawk-moth. **(deducing, inferring, drawing conclusions)**
- Look briefly at pages 4–7. Discuss each picture in turn and ask the children what is happening. Introduce the more challenging vocabulary, e.g. *dragonfly's* (p.5), *reply* (p.7). **(word reading, developing vocabulary)**
- Depending on your usual practice and the group you are working with, you may wish to:
  - Share the book with the children before they read it themselves.
  - Read the first few pages together and then ask the children to read the rest independently. In this case, read pages 4–7 with the children. What do the children notice about some of the words? (It uses rhyming text – *tree/Zee, eyes/dragonfly's, small/all, Hi!/reply*.) Ask the children to read on independently.
  - Invite the children to read the whole book independently.

> During reading

- If you have not already done so, ask the children what to do if they encounter a difficult word. Praise children who successfully decode unfamiliar words. Note the children's ability to read the common exception words.
- As you listen to individual children read, you may wish to ask might want to ask them to stop and summarize what has happened so far and predict what will happen next. **(summarizing, predicting)**
- As the children read, ask them to look out for capital letters.

Assessment point

Can the children read aloud and begin to use expression to show awareness of punctuation?

After reading

Returning to the text

- Ask the children what they thought of the story and the ending. **(personal response)**
- Ask the children to tell you briefly what happened in the story. **(recall, summarizing)**

Assessment point
Can the children retell known stories, including significant events/main ideas in sequence?

Developing comprehension

- Ask the children why Zee talked to Zak's back. **(deducing, inferring, drawing conclusions)**
- Discuss how Zee felt when he found out that he had been talking to Zak's back. **(empathizing)**
- Have the children ever felt as if someone has ignored them? How did they feel?

Assessment point
Can the children make plausible predictions about characters, using knowledge of the story own experiences, etc.?

Developing grammar, punctuation and spelling

- Turn to page 2. Discuss the use of a capital letter at the start of the names Zak and Zee. Now turn to page 8. Discuss the use of a capital letter for the personal pronoun I. Can the children give you other examples where capital letters are used?
- Turn to pages 10–11. Point out the words *tea*, *me*, and *Zee*. Can the children identify the letters in each word that make the /ee/ sound?

Developing fluency

- Ask one of the children to role play being Zee Bug and ask the other children to ask 'him' questions based on the experiences shown in the book. **(questioning, empathizing)**

In this story

Zak Bug

Zee Bug

❯ Follow-up

Writing activities

- Complete the *Match the rhyming words* Photocopy Master. **(short writing task)**
- Invite the children to write another story about Zak and Zee using the *Zak and Zee* Photocopy Master. **(longer writing task)**

Other literacy activities

- Challenge the children to tell the story from Zee's viewpoint. **(spoken language)**

Cross-curricular activities

- Make finger puppets of Zee and Zak and role play the story. **(Art and Design)**
- Find out more about insects that have 'eye' markings, e.g. peacock butterfly, eyed hawk-moth. **(Science)**
- Investigate the importance of eyes and identify which sense they are associated with. **(Science)**

Bug Hunt
BY CLAIRE LLEWELLYN

Curricula correlation

English National Curriculum

Spoken language	Use spoken language to develop understanding through speculating, hypothesising, imagining and exploring ideas
Word reading	Read words of more than one syllable
Comprehension	Understand books by discussing the significance of the title and events
	Draw on what they already know or on background information and vocabulary provided by the teacher

Phonics and vocabulary

Two-syllable words	flowers, feelers, earwig
Decodable words (Phase 4)	hunt, look, this, long, help, wing, rest, fast, night, glass, ever, flowers, feelers, earwig
Common exception words	do, one, what, like, have, about
Challenge and context words	ladybird, eight, spider, flies, house, stones, body

Developing grammar, punctuation and spelling

Grammar and Punctuation	Introduction to question marks to demarcate sentences	Do you like bugs? I do.
Spelling	New consonant spelling *wh* in question words	what, why

Reading assessment points

Word reading	Can the children recognise familiar words in simple texts?
Comprehension	Are the children beginning to make predictions based on titles, text, blurb and/or pictures?
	Can the children answer simple questions/find information in response to a direct, literal question?
	Are the children beginning to recognise a range of patterns in texts, including stories, rhymes and non-fiction?
	Can the children talk about likes/dislikes of stories and information texts?

Scottish Curriculum for Excellence

Listening and talking	I can show my understanding of what I listen to or watch by responding to and asking different kinds of questions LIT 1-07a
Reading	Using what I know about the features of different types of texts, I can find, select, sort and use information for a specific purpose LIT 1-14a
	To help me develop an informed view, I can recognise the difference between fact and opinion LIT 1-18a

Welsh National Literacy Framework

Oracy	Contribute to conversations and respond to others, taking turns when prompted (Collaboration and discussion)
Reading	Apply the following reading strategies with increasing independence: phonic strategies to decode words, recognition of high-frequency words, context clues, e.g. prior knowledge, graphic and syntactic clues, and self-correction, including re-reading and reading ahead (Reading strategies)
	Identify simple text features such as titles and pictures to indicate what the text is about (Reading strategies)

Northern Ireland Curriculum

Talking and Listening	Express themselves with increasing clarity and confidence, using a growing vocabulary and more complex sentence structure
Reading	Make and give reasons for predictions

About this book

Ant goes on a bug hunt in his house and garden. He finds a variety of minibeasts.

You will need

- *Minibeasts quiz* Photocopy Master, *Teaching Handbook* for Year I/P2
- *Label the minibeasts* Photocopy Master, *Teaching Handbook* for Year I/P2
- Magnifying glass and pictures of an earwig, ant, a ladybird, fly, moth and spider

Before reading

- Discuss with the children what they already know about Ant and his character. **(activating prior knowledge)**

- Look at the cover. Ask the children what Ant is doing. What kinds of bugs (minibeasts) do the children think Ant will find? **(predicting)**

- Look at page 3. What is Ant holding? What is it used for? Demonstrate how a magnifying glass is used. Then look at the pictures of the minibeasts (earwig, ant, ladybird, fly, moth and spider). Can the children name them? Where can these bugs be found? What kind of bugs do the children like? **(activating prior knowledge)**

Assessment point

Are the children beginning to make predictions based on titles, text, blurb and, or pictures?

Assessment point

Can the children recognise familiar words in simple texts?

Phonic opportunity

- Draw attention to the two-syllable words in the text: *earwig*, *feelers*, *flowers*. Model breaking these longer words down to help with decoding and blending.

- Alternatively, depending on the phonic work you have been undertaking, select other decodable words from the book and remind the children how to say and blend phonemes.

- You may also wish to point out some of the common exception words, or practise decoding some of the challenge and context words in this book.

- Depending on your usual practice and the group you are working with, you may wish to:
  - Share the book with the children before they read it themselves. Model pausing at new vocabulary and checking meaning.
  - Read a few pages together and ask the children to read the rest independently. In this case, read pages 4 and 5 together as these contain some new vocabulary. Then ask the children to read the book independently.
  - Invite the children to read the whole book independently.

> During reading

- If you have not already done so, ask the children what to do if they encounter a difficult word. Praise children who successfully decode unfamiliar words.
- As you listen to individual children you may wish to ask some of the following questions to check their understanding of the book:
  - Where did Ant hunt for bugs? (p.3)
  - How many legs does an earwig have?
  - What does it use its feelers for? (p.5)
  - What does Ant say about the fly? (p.10)
- Show the children and example of a question mark ("*I wonder why?*", p.8). Ask them to look out for more examples as they read through the book.

Assessment point

Can the children answer simple questions/find information in response to a direct, literal question?

After reading

Returning to the text

- Ask the children what they thought of the book and which part they enjoyed most. Why? **(personal response)**

- What is it that shows this is a non-fiction book rather than a story book? Discuss why people read and write non-fiction books and magazines (for information, enjoyment) and ask the children to give you personal examples. You may need to discuss the fictional figure (Ant) and point out he is not involved in a story in this book but is being used for a factual purpose. **(deducing, inferring, drawing conclusions)**

> **Assessment point**
> Can the children talk about likes/dislikes of stories and information texts?

> **Assessment point**
> Are the children beginning to recognise a range of patterns in texts, including stories, rhymes and non-fiction?

Developing comprehension

- Ask the children:
  - Does Ant like bugs? How do you know?
  - Where did he find the earwig, ant, ladybird, fly, moth and the spider?
  - Why was the moth sleeping?
  (recall, deducing, inferring, drawing conclusions)

Look at these flowers.
What can you see?
It is a ladybird.

Developing vocabulary

- What are the things called that are on the ant's head? If the children in the group know the word 'antennae', this might be a good opportunity to introduce it as an alternative to feelers.
- Play the *What am I?* game. This could be played in pairs or as a whole group. Model the activity by giving one or two clues about one of the minibeasts, e.g. This bug has six legs and two eyes. It likes leaves. (earwig) The children try to guess which minibeast you are describing.
- Then, ask the children, in pairs, to devise their own clues about a minibeast and invite each pair to say their clues so that the rest of the group can guess the minibeast. **(spoken language)**

Developing grammar, punctuation and spelling

- Look at the examples of question marks the children have found. Look at the sentences that feature this punctuation mark and check that they understand that these are questions. Can they think of their own question to ask that would need a question mark at the end? Check that the children understand the difference between exclamation marks and question marks.
- Look at the question words *what*, *where* and *why*. Can the children identify which letters make the /w/ sound? Discuss how two letters ('wh') make one sound here.

❯ Follow-up

Writing activities

- Use the *Minibeasts quiz* Photocopy Master. **(longer writing task)**
- Children could complete the *Label the minibeasts* Photocopy Master. **(short writing task)**

Cross-curricular activities

- Go on a minibeast hunt. How many different minibeasts can the children find? Make a graph/pictogram. **(Science, Maths)**
- Build an 'insect': children could design the parts of an insect and then assemble them. **(DT)**
- Sort a set of minibeast pictures. Children could decide their own categories. **(Maths, Science)**

What Do Bugs Eat?
BY HAYDN MIDDLETON

Curricula correlation

English National Curriculum

Spoken language	Articulate and justify answers, arguments and opinions
Word reading	Respond speedily with the correct sound to graphemes for all 40+ phonemes
Comprehension	Explain clearly their understanding of what is read to them
	Understand books by discussing the significance of the title and events

Phonics and vocabulary

Adjacent consonants	drink, plant, hunt, small, jump, from
Decodable words (Phase 4)	bigger, into, remember, contents, food, drink, from, plant, fur, jump, rolls, hunt, small
Common exception words	do, what, some, something
Challenge and context words	ladybird, spider, aphids, beetle, fleas, locust, blood, bite, eat, water bear, whose

Developing grammar, punctuation and spelling

Grammar and Punctuation	Separation of words with spaces	Good example on page 14.
	How words can combine to make sentences	
Spelling	The sound /ee/ spelt as ea	fleas, eat, team

Reading assessment points

Word reading	Can the children use phonic knowledge to attempt unknown words?
Comprehension	Are the children beginning to make predictions based on titles, text, blurb and/or pictures?
	Are the children beginning to recognise a range of patterns in texts, including stories, rhymes and non-fiction?
	Can the children talk about likes/dislikes of stories and information texts?
	Can the children, with support, find information to help answer simple, literal questions, in texts at an appropriate reading level?

Scottish Curriculum for Excellence

Listening and talking	I can select ideas and relevant information, organise these in a logical sequence and use words which will be interesting and/or useful for others LIT 1-06a
Reading	To help me develop an informed view, I can recognise the difference between fact and opinion LIT 1-18a
	Using what I know about the features of different types of texts, I can find, select, sort and use information for a specific purpose LIT 1-14a

Welsh National Literacy Framework

Oracy	Express an opinion on familiar subjects (Speaking)
Reading	Apply the following reading strategies with increasing independence: phonic strategies to decode words, recognition of high-frequency words, context clues, e.g. prior knowledge, graphic and syntactic clues, and self-correction, including re-reading and reading ahead (Reading strategies)
	Identify simple text features such as titles and pictures to indicate what the text is about (Reading strategies)
	Recall details from information texts (Comprehension)

Northern Ireland Curriculum

Talking and Listening	Express themselves with increasing clarity and confidence, using a growing vocabulary and more complex sentence structure
Reading	Make and give reasons for predictions

What Do Bugs Eat?

About this book

This non-fiction text looks at a variety of bugs (minibeasts) and what they eat.

You will need
- *Match the bug to its food* Photocopy Master, *Teaching Handbook* for Year 1/P2
- *My favourite bug* Photocopy Master, *Teaching Handbook* for Year 1/P2

▶ Before reading

- Look at the cover of the book. Ask the children if they can guess what the bug is. Together, read the title and the back cover blurb. What is the book about? Do the children have any ideas about how a small bug could eat a bigger bug? **(activating prior knowledge, predicting)** ≪≪≪

Assessment point
Are the children beginning to make predictions based on titles, text, blurb and/or pictures?

- Read the contents page. How do we use a contents page? Ask the children to tell you the page where they can find information about the water bear (p.10) and the dung beetle (p.12). **(developing fluency)**

- Look briefly at pages 4, 8, 9 and 13. Discuss each picture in turn and read the text, focusing on the more challenging vocabulary: *spider* (p.4), *fleas* (p.8), *blood* (p.8), *locust*, *team* (p.15). **(developing vocabulary)**

- Depending on your usual practice and the group you are working with, you may wish to:
  - ☐ Share the book with the children before they read it themselves.
  - ☐ Read the opening pages together and ask the children to read the rest independently.
  - ☐ Invite the children to read the whole book independently.

Phonic opportunity

- Draw attention to words with adjacent consonants: *hunt, jump, from, drink, plant*. Read one of the words, sound it out and demonstrate how to blend the adjacent consonants. Ask the children to identify and blend the separate consonant sounds in one of the other words.
- Alternatively, depending on the phonic work you have been undertaking, select one or two of the words from the book and remind the children how to say and blend phonemes.
- You may also wish to point out some of the common exception words, or practise decoding some of the challenge and context words in this book.

Assessment point
Can the children use phonic knowledge to attempt unknown words?

This cat has fleas on its fur.
The fleas will bite the cat.
Then they drink its blood.

Fleas can jump on to you.
Then they drink *your* blood.

During reading

- If you have not already done so, ask the children what to do if they encounter a difficult word, modelling with an example from the book if necessary. Remind the children of the more challenging vocabulary which you looked at before reading the book.
- As you listen to individual children read, you may wish to ask some of the following questions to check their understanding of the book:
  - How does the spider capture the fly? (p.4)
  - What do fleas drink? (pp.8–9)
  - How big is a water bear? (p.10)
  - What does a dung beetle eat?
  - What is dung? (p.13)

> **Assessment point**
> Can the children, with support, find information to help answer simple, literal questions, in texts at an appropriate reading level?

After reading

Returning to the text

- Ask the children what they thought of the book and which were the most interesting pages. **(personal response)**
- What tells the children that this book is a non-fiction book rather than a story book? Discuss why people read and write non-fiction books and magazines (information, enjoyment). What would people learn from reading this book? **(deducing, inferring, drawing conclusions)**

> **Assessment point**
> Are the children beginning to recognise a range of patterns in texts, including stories, rhymes and non-fiction?

Developing comprehension

- Look at pages 10 and 11 together. Ask the children why these minibeasts are called 'water bears'. **(inferring, deducing)**
- What do scientists have to use to be able to see the bugs?
- Read pages 14 and 15. How do the ants manage to eat a bigger bug?
- Look at page 16. Can the children match each bug to what it eats? **(recall)**
- Which is the children's favourite bug in the book? Why? **(personal response)**

Assessment point
Can the children talk about likes/dislikes of stories and information texts?

Developing grammar, punctuation and spelling

- Look at how sentences are written. Turn to page 14 and point out the spaces between the words and the order that they words are in so the sentence makes sense. Write a sentence and then jumble the words. Does the sentence still make sense?
- Turn to page 2. Point out the word *eat*. Can the children identify the letters that make the /ee/ sound?

❯ Follow-up

Writing activities

- Ask the children to match the minibeast to the food it eats, using the *Match the bug to its food* Photocopy Master. **(short writing task)**
- Children could write about their favourite minibeast from the book. Why do the children like this creature? What does it eat? Can the children find out one more fact about their minibeast and write it in the 'Did you know?' box on the *My favourite bug* Photocopy Master? **(longer writing task)**

Cross-curricular activities

- Sort and classify the different bugs/minibeasts. How many legs do they have? Do they have wings? What do they eat? Where do they live? **(Science, Maths)**
- Children could paint or make one of the minibeasts, e.g. ladybird, water bear, dung beetle, flea. **(Art and Design, DT)**